All Kinds of Families

Written by Anita Ganeri

Illustrated by Ayesha Rubio
and Jenny Palmer

CRABTREE
PUBLISHING COMPANY
WWW.CRABTREEBOOKS.COM

CRABTREE
PUBLISHING COMPANY
WWW.CRABTREEBOOKS.COM

Author: Anita Ganeri

Editorial director: Kathy Middleton

Editors: Nicola Edwards, Ellen Rodger

Illustrators: Ayesha Rubio, Jenny Palmer

Proofreader: Crystal Sikkens

Designer: Little Red Ant

Prepress technician: Margaret Salter

Print coordinator: Katherine Berti

Library and Archives Canada Cataloguing in Publication

Title: All kinds of families / written by Anita Ganeri ; illustrated by
  Ayesha Rubio and Jenny Palmer.
Names: Ganeri, Anita, 1961- author. | Rubio, Ayesha L., illustrator. |
  Palmer, Jenny (Illustrator), illustrator.
Description: Series statement: All kinds of people |
  Previously published: London: Franklin Watts, 2019. |
  Includes index.
Identifiers: Canadiana (print) 20190200537 |
  Canadiana (ebook) 20190200545 |
  ISBN 9780778768029 (hardcover) |
  ISBN 9780778768067 (softcover) |
  ISBN 9781427124234 (HTML)
Subjects: LCSH: Families—Juvenile literature.
Classification: LCC HQ744 .G36 2020 | DDC j306.85—dc23

Library of Congress Cataloging-in-Publication Data

Names: Ganeri, Anita, 1961- author. | Lopez Rubio, Ayesha,
  illustrator.
Title: All kinds of families / written by Anita Ganeri ; illustrated by
  Ayesha Rubio and Jenny Palmer.
Description: New York, NY : Crabtree Publishing Company, 2020. |
  Series: All kinds of people | Includes index.
Identifiers: LCCN 2019043930 (print) | LCCN 2019043931 (ebook)
  ISBN 9780778768029 (hardcover) |
  ISBN 9780778768067 (paperback) |
  ISBN 9781427124234 (ebook)
Subjects: LCSH: Families--Juvenile literature.
Classification: LCC HQ519 .G365 2020 (print) | LCC HQ519 (ebook) |
  DDC 306.85--dc23
LC record available at https://lccn.loc.gov/2019043930
LC ebook record available at https://lccn.loc.gov/2019043931

Crabtree Publishing Company
www.crabtreebooks.com   1-800-387-7650
Published by Crabtree Publishing Company in 2020

Published in Canada
Crabtree Publishing
616 Welland Avenue
St. Catharines, ON
L2M 5V6

Published in the United States
Crabtree Publishing
PMB 59051
350 Fifth Ave, 59th Floor
New York, NY 10118

Printed in the U.S.A./012020/CG20191115

First published in Great Britain in 2019 by The Watts Publishing Group
Copyright © The Watts Publishing Group 2019

Contents

There are all kinds of families.

We live with our grandparents.

I have two moms.

Families come in all shapes and sizes.

I live with my parents, aunts, uncles, and cousins.

4

Some families
live together.

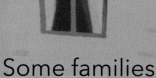

In my house,
there's my mom,
dad, sister,
brother, and me.

My dad works in
a different country.
I talk to him on the
computer.

Some families
live apart.

What is your family like?

5

Some children live with two parents. A lot of children live with a mom and a dad.

Some children have two moms, while others have two dads.

Some children live with just one parent.

This can be just their mom, or just their dad.

Sometimes, moms and dads can't live together. They split up or they may get **divorced**. One of them may move away and live somewhere else.

When my mom and dad split up, my dad went to live in the next town.

Some children share their time between their mom and dad. The parent who has moved away is still part of their family.

We live with our mom during the week, and go to our dad's house on weekends.

If your parents split up, your mom or dad might find another **partner** and get married. Their new partner may become your stepdad or stepmom.

Your stepmom or stepdad might have their own children. Then, you all become part of the same family.

This can feel strange at first.
You might feel shy or upset.

But when you get to know each other,
it can be fun to have more people to
talk to and spend time with.

Some children live separately from their grandparents, uncles, aunts, and cousins. They may live close to each other or far away.

I like visiting my grandma and grandpa.

Sometimes the whole family lives together in the same place.

Our house is really busy and noisy. But there's always someone to talk to if you feel lonely.

There are all kinds of ways
of making a family.

We have a cake to
celebrate the day I
was adopted.

Some children are **adopted**. This means they
cannot live with their birth family. A new family is
chosen for them. This is their forever family.

Some children are adopted when they are babies. Some children are adopted when they are older.

My mom and dad adopted me first. Then they adopted my brother.

Some children go to live with a **foster family**. They may stay there for a few weeks or a few years. Afterward, they may go back to their birth family or be adopted.

This is my foster family. Like many families, we all enjoy doing different things.

The foster family may have other children staying with them. They may have their own children living with them, as well.

This is my bedroom. I sleep on the top bunk.

Families can be very big. Some children have a lot of brothers...or a lot of sisters...or a lot of sisters and brothers.

Some families are very small. A family may have only two people in it, but it is still a family.

Some children are **only children**. They don't have any brothers or sisters.

All families argue sometimes.

Sometimes different people have different feelings about things.

But these feelings can change quickly.

Being part of a happy family means feeling safe, loved, and looked after.

It also means feeling happy to come home.

Everyday life in a family can be very busy, especially at breakfast time.

Some parents go to work. They rush around getting ready, getting the children to school, and getting to work on time.

Most children go to school, but some are too young. They may go to a daycare, babysitter, or to their grandparents. Some may stay home with their mom or dad.

After school, some children go to an after-school club or daycare until their parents come home from work.

Being part of a family can be a lot of fun.

Some families go on vacation. They might fly on an airplane. They might go to the beach and dig in the sand. They might visit a theme park. They might just stay home and snuggle up in front of the TV.

Some families love to celebrate special days. These might be birthdays, weddings, or festivals, such as Christmas, Baisakhi, Eid, Diwali, or Hanukkah.

Often, these are times when all the family gets together, even if they live far apart.

Who is in your family—moms, dads, aunts, uncles, cousins, grandparents? But families are much more than these.

My mom's best friend is like my auntie.

We go on vacation with our neighbors.

Good friends and neighbors can be very important members of your family. You feel like a part of their family, as well.

Some people have pet cats, dogs, rabbits, and even stick insects. Their pets count as part of their family.

I buy my pets a present on their birthday.

Families can change over time.

Sometimes, new members are added to a family and it gets bigger. This happens when a new baby is born, or someone gets married.

Sometimes, a member of the family dies and the family gets smaller. There are all kinds of families. They can be big, small, loud, or quiet. They may live together, or far away. They argue, and make up.

Every family is different. So, what is your family like?

Notes for teachers, parents, and caregivers

This book introduces children to the topic of families, and the many ways in which families may be put together and change over time. The book aims to show children that there is no such thing as a "normal" family. Families come in all shapes and sizes—single-parent, single-sex, blended families, foster and adoptive families, and so on.

You may find it useful to start a discussion about different kinds of families by talking about your child's own family, and the families of their friends. You could then encourage them to find out more about their family, and put the information together as a family tree, with small artwork portraits or photographs.

Coping with changes

Changes in family life, such as divorce or remarriage, can be extremely unsettling and confusing experiences for children. It is important to allow children time to talk about how they are feeling and ask any questions. Be honest about what is happening, though what you say will inevitably depend on the age of the child. Acknowledge that they may be feeling frightened or sad, but stress that they are still loved, and that both of their parents will continue to look after them.

Showing support in adoption

Some families are formed by adoption, and this can raise many questions both from the adopted child, and from their classmates and other friends. An adopted child might feel upset if their friends tease them because they are adopted. It is important to talk to them about adoption, and to suggest ways for them to handle any negative comments. It might also be worth suggesting to your school that they talk to students about adoption, and the importance of inclusion, more generally, without singling any individual child out.

Websites for Parents and Educators

www.kidshelpphone.ca
Advice and support 24 hours a day, seven days a week for young people with any issue they may be going through.

www.211.org

A website that helps families connect with services for help in all of the United States and most of Canada.

www.adopt.org/
Support for all those parenting or supporting children who cannot live with their birth parents.

www.relate.org.uk/
Helping people of all ages and backgrounds strengthen their relationships.

Useful words

adopted   To become part of a family that you were not born into

divorce   When two people end their marriage

foster family   A family in which children are cared for by people who are not their parents

homesick   The feeling of missing home very much when you are away from it

only child   A child in a family who does not have brothers or sisters

partner   Each person in a couple

Index